A Ground More Arable

The poet posing for posterity in front of Grandfather's house.

A Ground More Arable

New Poems

Don Gutteridge

Wet Ink Books

First Edition

Wet Ink Books
www.WetInkBooks.com
WetInkBooks@gmail.com

A Ground More Arable
by Don Gutteridge

Cover Image – www.clipart.com with permission
Cover Design – Richard M. Grove
Layout and Design – Richard M. Grove

Typeset in Garamond
Printed and bound in Canada
Distributed in USA by Ingram,
          – to set up an account to order this or any Ingram book call – 1-800-937-0152

Library and Archives Canada Cataloguing in Publication

Title: A ground more arable : new poems / Don Gutteridge.
Names: Gutteridge, Don, 1937- author.
Identifiers: Canadiana 20230443206 | ISBN 9781989786895 (softcover)
Classification: LCC PS8513.U85 G76 2023 | DDC C811/.54—dc23

Contents

Grandpa, Shaving

On Saturday mornings, I crept
downstairs and turned
my ten-year, yearning
eyes upon Grandfather,
shaving, entranced by the way
the soft-bristled brush,
breathing steam, whipped up
a lather in the blue bowl,
like eddies of froth purring
on a pond, and slathered it
on the rough stubble of cheeks
and chin and the brisk whiskers
above the lip that looped
his smile, and O what a wonder
as he guided the razor in
and around and over with the elan
of a blind man cruising
the bailiwicks of Braille, and when
he was done and his face shone,
I knew, even then,
that moments like these come only
when something is stirred in the soul.

Long-Legged

O how we loved to ogle
the girls and their long-legged
leaping over Grandfather's
lawn, like propelled gazelles
outbounding the lion's bounce,
and O the dithyrambic
dance of their double-Dutch
and their tiptoe touch on the
hopscotched walk, and the bevel
and yaw of their tawny bodies
(frocks and frillies abloom
in the breeze), but when they went
cartwheeling, thigh over thigh,
something more aboding
than curiosity corrupted
our gaze, and fostered there.

Sunday Morning Cinema

For John

After an evening's fete
of rye-and-ginger and smoke-
gets-in-your-eye, it is Dad's
turn to feed the bairns
breakfast, and so, nursing
the throb, hobnobbing
in my head, I navigate the stairs
warily, and find you sitting
solo before the telly,
bright-eyed and good-
to-go, watching the frantic
antics of Abbott and Costello,
with the volume amped up
loud enough to stun a buffalo
and his cousins, and you pat the soft
spot beside you and give me
a greeter's grin, as if to say
you're glad to have my company,
fuzzy-tongued or not.

Hellzapoppin'

For my grandfather in loving memory

My grandfather attended
but two movies in his lifetime:
Hellzapoppin' and the *Al
Jolson Story,* the former, a farrago
of pratfalls and leering pirouettes,
the latter, a soulful songfest
with Larry Parks unabashed
in blackface, but every Saturday
at supper, after my afternoon
of sagebrush sagas, Gramps
would listen to my scene-by-scene
exegesis, as if he were
on speaking terms with Hoppy
or Tex or a yodeling Gene,
or was, perhaps, a cinema-intimate.

The Knack

That misbegotten summer,
the rumour of rude doings
in Hendries' henhouse
shocked and appalled (in equal
numbers), when Jo-Anne
reportedly dropped her drawers,
lay down on her buttocked back
and let her thighs sigh,
and the biggest bloke in the room,
who knew a lot more about
hanky-panky than the tittering
striplings nearby (gawking
in clotted awe), stepped
right up and in, as she fluttered
her flanks and prayed he had
the knack – but the torpid tale
may have lost much
of its mustard in the tawdry
retelling.

Body-and-Soul

I'd like to think that some-
where we are all immortal
in a place where the good gods
grin and forgive, where some
semblance of what we once were,
abides and breathes, a sanctuary
for the solace of souls, where we can
recall everything we've un-
remembered, and those we loved
till our bones bled and surrendered
to Death's dominion, bind up
our wounds, and even though
we may believe in Heaven's
leavening or the gift of its grace,
body-and-soul will find
a way to come uncoupled
and grieve on their own.

Kissing Your Sister

For Shirley McCord

Whenever we chose to play
Spin the Bottle, and the love-
jug swayed and pointed
to Shirley (my girl-next-door
with pigtails that jiggled
and freckles like nuggets of nougat)
I bade her buckle up
to the bliss in my lips, but, alas,
despite the ardor of my pardon-me
pucker, it felt as if
I were kissing my sister.

Jinned

O how we loved to run
with the wind bevelling our backs,
dishevelled in our hair, the girls
beside us with their long-legged
allure and antic prancing,
and if our arms were wings,
we would fly like Icarus
too close to the sun
just to feel the fathoms
of our freefalling bodies,
our bones afloat in the flotsam
of their flesh, and here, where the sky
thrives, we are glad to be guests
of the gods and like the poets
of old, go mad in the wind-
jinned, fancy-fed
fury of their making.

Strewn Ruins

Point Edward: 1947

When Parson Bell's manse
blew up like Little Pig's
straw abode, scattering
lath and plaster and stricken
bricks everywhere at once,
and we arrived five minutes
behind the fire brigade
in time to see the dust
settle like a dancer's petticoats,
we thought of bomb-bursts
on the Somme or the slow explosion
of a hand-tossed grenade
or perhaps some boulder-buckling
ruckus in Hell, and wondered
idly whether the match
intended for cigarette or cigar
was still attached to the man
who lit it.

Litmus

What I remember most
about the War, besides
the empty chair at suppertime
where, I was told, my father
would someday sit in his blue
tunic and buffed brass,
or the pink Savings stamps
that wouldn't stick for a nickel
or a dime, or gathering milk-
weed floss to keep
a sailor's jacket jaunty
with its feathered flotsam, was my Gran
in the downstairs kitchen,
knitting three-needled
Argyle socks for her overseas
sons and an extra pair
for a good buddy, to keep
their toes from tingling and their hearts
cozied, her lips moving,
stitch by numbing stitch,
as if in penitent prayer
or some ancient incantation
of mothers everywhere to the gods
who suffered their sons to bleed
and perish beyond the healing
ambit of their love.

Boulevards

For Sandy, again

Whenever I thought about girls,
and often, they were always
beautiful, blond-locked,
and waiting to be rescued,
and I was their dallying Galahad,
my feelings lofty, but that serene
summer, you swam blue-eyed
into view, flesh-and-blood
and very not blond, needing
nothing from a lover but a hand
to hold or lips to seal a kiss,
and so we strolled the home-
boulevards, without a haw
or a hem, very much in love
with love, and as real as a jeweller's
gems.

How Like a Cherub

For Tom in loving memory

How like a cherub you look,
plumped in your child's chair
with cheeks the colour roses
wished they were, your locks
a heftier red Van Gogh
would approve, your infant's chin
a just-done dumpling,
and your baby-fists as wee
and squeezed as a jockey's socks,
and if the sky should ever
choose to boast a better
blue, your eyes and the smile
they glorify will nicely do,
and O how I long to have you
here forever like this:
a mangered angel too perfect
for God's applause.

Wistful

S.S. No. 12, Sarnia Township: 1949
For Janice and Ronnie Young

His mother may have called him
"Ronnie," but to the rest of us,
who were the unwitting patrons
of his patter, he was just "Mouth,"
a likely lad, who delivered
his salty, loose-lipped
quips and a daily recounting
of his sister's amorous attributes
with a snide and a leer that kept
our cloakroom stoked,
but whenever I happened to glance
her way, two rows
over, all I noticed
was the halo of her hair, as blond
as a Boedecian beauty, and the wistful
look that bedizened her eyes.

Toddler-Logic

For Tim

Long before you could read
a word or tell a Jedi
from a gerbil, you could
recite the opening spiel
from *Star Wars,* as if
you had written it yourself
as a favour to George Lucas,
and although it was set in a
galaxy far far away,
there was something in the
lightsaber's slash
and moon-dodging rockets
and cloak-robed Obi
and Buddha-browed Yoda
and the ever-devious Darth
that appealed to your toddler-logic,
while mine was a tepid tour
with the likes of Buck Rogers
in his space togs, or blond-
locked Flash Gordon
or Dick Tracy's flickering
wrist or Mandrake flogging
magic with a cut of his cape,
but boys everywhere, then
or now, with their dewy-eyed
zeal, will always be dazzled
by the glamour of galaxies far
enough away to be real.

O Frabjous Day

A frabjous day on Canatara's
crystalline sands: when the wind
howled like a horse-whipped
cripple and breakers teethed
on the beleaguered beach with a
roar like tympanis in tantrum,
while the sun hung above us,
like a bloated bloom in the blue
vase of the sky, and we paused,
in our afternoons' doing,
long enough to feel the wind
flinch on the skin, and let all
that boisterous Beauty, in.

For King and Country

Remembrance Day: 2022
For my grandfather in loving memory

On this day I remember
to remember my grandfather
and his long-ago war,
when cousin fought cousin
in hand-to-hand combat
in rain-drenched trenches,
mudded with their blood, and Death
was a bayonet in the belly
or a shard of shrapnel, fluttering
the gut, and the King and Country
he'd abandoned for better days
abroad, were still enough
to waken the will to kill,
and I wonder, as he lay thrice-
wounded, praying the next
breath would last, if he thought
of the son he'd never seen,
or dreamed of me, tucked
and nuzzled in a womb, no bigger
than a wombat's begat.

Yes

Guelph, Ontario: 1961
For Anne in loving memory

I'd planned to pop the question
on bended knee, but when
that nuptial thought bubbled up,
you and I were seated
side by side in your soft-
topped Volks, where genuflection
was a risky option, but the moon-
light seemed propitious,
winking winsome in the winter-
carved dark, and the stars
blinked above it like the Queen's
sequins, but the words I'd rehearsed
came out in reverse, and I said,
in my nevertheless patter,
without preamble or poise,
"We ought to get married," and you,
doing your best to look
unstartled, said yes.

Tagging Along

For my father in loving memory

My Dad lets me tag along
on a cold March morning
while he sets his muskrat traps
in the wind-whetted shallows
of Mitchell's Bay, placing
each baited barb
below the water-line,
just so (like a card-shark
carny beguiling the marks)
where the hapless rodents,
coming up for air and a bite
of breakfast, find themselves
to be the bitten, their silken
coats agleam in the sunlight
that warms their passing, their velvet
pelts destined to be draped
on milady's homely shoulders.

Tomfoolery

For John

After a hard night's
partying, it was my turn
to make breakfast for my son,
and we sat together on the
chesterfield, staring at the
Abbott and Costello show
on our blurred black-and-white,
me: through my hangover haze
and you with wide-eyed
delight, as the comic duo
dazzled us with their "Who's on First?"
fandango – Abbott, like a slim,
mustachioed lothario,
delivering his impertinent ripostes
with Gatling-gun gusto,
while Costello, like an under-plumped
dumpling, parried them with jowled
bewilderment, and O how you
howled (when the giggles allowed)
at such divine drollery,
such cosmic tomfoolery.

On the Road

Chatham, Ontario: 1957

Long before the snows
clothed our road and made it
sled-friendly, we set up,
on a far, dead-end
acre, our makeshift net
with its burlap bulge and stalwart
struts, and we wielded our tooth-
pick sticks and bouncy-
ball puck, as if it were
Hockey Night in Canada
and we were winter warriors
foraging in the Forum for goals
and hat-trick glory, that is,
until some impudent blimp
of an auto with no respect
for junior jocks, bullied
into view and, outscored,
we skedaddled, pursued by boos
and catcalls from the female fans
a-gawk on the walk.

Where Poppies Blow

November 11, 2022

Whenever I hear those luminous
lines recited by some aging,
badge-breasted vet
beside a wreathe-wrapped
cenotaph, the molten notes
of the Last Post still
ringing in his ears, I see
the fields of Flanders teeming
with poppies, and every blood-
red bloom somebody's
remembrance, soothed anew
by McCrae's consoling tropes
and the honey-touch of a perfect
poem.

First Flight

For my father in loving memory

My Dad thinks it's time I flew
and I agree, picturing
swans swooning on a sea-
breeze that weaves their wings
aloft, and there on the tarmac
squats an antique two-seater
that ought to have been pensioned off
or sold for scrap, but we buckle in
like Bader and his batman,
the engine coughs like a gassed
asthmatic, and the solitary prop
opts to spin like a lop-
sided baton, grips the wind
in its tongued teeth and sends us
bounding down the runway
like a drunk doing a debonaire's
dance, and *mirabile dictu*
we're afloat, my father and me,
two peas from the family
pod, on eddies of air
wuthering above us and below,
a stone's throw from God's
abode, a *tabula rasa*
I will write the joys of
this day upon.

Ode to Sappho

Sappho! I see you now
on that Leucadian cliff,
the hot Sicilian sun
besotting on your brow, and I wonder,
in the midst of your long exile,
how much you remember of Lesbos
and the graphic slant of its Grecian
light or those prim-limbed
girls you taught by day
and satisfied by night, loving
the way their bodies bloomed
under the tutelage of your touch
and the pebbled ebbing of its after-
math, and did you limn a homo-
erotic ode to all things
Vestal and Venusian before
you flung yourself and a thousand
unsung songs into the sea?

Wednesdays

The self-dubbed "Sarnia
Golf and Country Club"
sprawled obscenely green
across the sacred acreage
of our home-ground, all
nine holes of manicured
meadow, like a hooted rebuke
to those of us who had
to watch the city-physicians
(who shut up shop every
Wednesday at noon on the dot)
strolling the poached fairways
with caddies abaft, like Pooh-Bahs
and their kowtowing toadies,
while we were left to comb
the rough and ready in quest
of wayward balls we'd sell back
to the duffers for a dime, and some
of us even dreamt we might
one day ourselves become
pill-hawking doctors,
and while away our Wednesdays
in style.

Hooligans

We called it Fright Night,
but, truth to tell,
we wouldn't say "Boo!"
to the Holy Ghost or growl
behind out rubber-writhing
masks, as we prowled from door
to door like cat-burglars
on a break-and-enter binge,
ringing bells and soaping
windows, and whooping back
into the seamless dark,
our bravado intact, and somewhere
further afield, our country
brothers were tipping privies,
tossing tractors and spooking
paddocked cattle, while we,
like moon-soothed hooligans,
were happy to be making
illicit mischief.

All Hallows

Point Edward: October 30, 1944

It was Halloween eve, and there
we were chanting ah-
ki-lahs and counting cub-
badges on our cub-green
beanies and bobbing for apples
in a buckled tub, and on
my way home I was surprised
to find myself hobbling,
my left ankle pinched
stiff, prismed with pain,
and by the time I stumbled
onto Grandfather's lawn,
my body was alive with some-
thing alien and striving,
and the first fingerlings of fever
blistered on my brow –
and it would be one
heart-harrowing night
of sulfa-suffusions and seven
months abed and adrift
in my dreams before I found
my sea-legs again
danced home on All
Hallows Eve.

Larger-Than-Life

My high school teachers
were larger than life characters
whom Dickens would have borrowed
for comic relief:
Mr. Bond
who stalked the room, tossing
chalk like a one-armed juggler;
Mr. Marcy
who scrawled quadratics on the board
that might have been written in Sanskrit
and whose chief pedagogical principle
was "Scare 'em first" and then "Learn 'em;."
Mr. Ritchie
who preferred surnames and the
precise nicety of alphabetized seating;
Mr. Orr
who recited his war stories
to hushed youngsters, of being
'coned' over an ack-acking Berlin;
Miss Carter
arthritic-hipped, bereft
of breath, wobbling up three
flights to her eyrie – between wheezes;
Mr. Anderson
whose lab-jacket was acid-
splashed and Bunsen-burned;
and I knew even then at fourteen
that I would write them and their ilk
into the silken skein
of my poems and stories.

A Word in a Poem

A word in a poem is not
an approximate thought, it makes
its meaning with exact tact
and carries in its furled fury
just enough weight to rouse
or placate, and in its singular
syllable is housed a world.

Ecstatic

Ah, Catullus, you waxed
ecstatic about the whims
and wiles of Rome's women
in a language originally cast
for the likes of Virgil's homiletic
epic or Caesar's ponderous
Commentary – in images
and suppled couplets that saluted
the body and its unpolluted
beauty, with titillating wit,
ribald rhyme and a sly
eye on the ultimate prize,
and centuries on, despite
the rupturing upshot of Time,
we can still be un-annulled
by these Catullian theses
on love and sexual surrender.

Balm

Every evening when I was a
summer shy of seven,
before my bed could claim me
for sleep, I would slip downstairs
to say "sweet dreams"
to my Grandpa, and found him,
as ever, at ease in his soft-
bottomed rocker, the only
light in the room, that which
seeped in from the kitchen,
where Gran was counting stitches,
and the hunched console in the corner
with the orange throb in its throat
was pouring out the dreadful
news of the day, and I wondered
if his thoughts were drifting
towards the long-ago war
he'd weathered or the one on the radio,
where his sons now fought –
beyond the balm of his loving

Guzzle

My Gran was against the booze
and the Beveridge Rooms
that parlayed it for a nickel a draft
and one lick to a customer,
served in an eight-ounce
glass, topped up to the 'tide-
line,' to be consumed
solo and whole at a tassel-
free table, whilst sitting
down on a hard-boiled
chair designed to keep
your linger brief, and waiting
for the 'slinger' to bring the next
frothing effusion across
the floor that nobody but him
was permitted to wander upon,
as if the sole purpose
of a boozing afternoon
was to park your fanny on a
beer-parlour pew,
guzzle till you're stewed, and go.

Din

May 8, 1945

The week following my seven-
month fever-confinement
and my rousing return to school,
the War was declared to be over,
and when the doors were flung
wide, we raced like a runaway
tide into the din of church
bells and sirens and teeming,
gleeful streets, and I loped
home on legs still
learning the length of their leap,
ululating like an un-
distraught Castrati.
"We won! We won! We won!"
not knowing, then, that such
affairs, beyond our ken
or hopes, are never done.

Chaplin's Spats

Point Edward: July 31, 1947

It was the one misbegotten
night of the year when the
moon loomed, and witches
hitched a ride on borrowed
brooms and buzzed the country-
side, and goblins bobbed
out of the star-jarred dark,
and ghosts roamed in rippled
robes and booed, and bats
fattened on something
heathen in the breeze, and I
went waltzing door-to-door
in my Charlie Chaplin spats
and ersatz moustache – with a bagful
of goodies, a delicious shiver
in the bole of my bones, and a nod
to the Bogeyman dancing
with Doom.

Classical

Long before I'd come upon
Keats's life-extoling
odes, Mistress Rowley,
with her one wandering eye,
conducted a master class
in the poets of ancient Rome
(exulting in their Latinate lustre)
for the benefit of her monolingual
charges: the rolling Alexandrines
of Virgil's *Aeneid* with its stress
on the antepenultimate syllable
that sent the dactyls dancing,
or the lush lyrics of Catullian
love, bringing blushes
to both sides of our gendered
aisles, or the epistolary wit
and iambs of Horace we resurrected
one hexameter at a time
(happy he found home
in his Sabine abode), and for better
or worse, these were the first
poets to stir in me
the possibility of putting
words to work for something
already singing within.

Socrates

You took a lot of lip
from Xantippe, but nothing
in her low-slung tongue
could give pause to your daily
barefoot strolling among
look-a-like scholars,
upstart Atticans and couth
youth, eager to be
victims of your arresting questions,
your boggling interrogatives,
and you cared not
that you were blimp-bellied
with a nose like a much-punched
pugilist, for yours was a life
lived in the mind, where truth
has its own terrain, and in
the end, your impious whims
brought you to hemlock
and the slow dredging of every
thought you'd left behind
for Plato to make Socratical.

Berry-Bright

For Tom in loving memory

In a long-forgotten drawer
I find this full-colour
photo of you at a year
and a tad, straddling your berry-
bright Tonka (because
your plump unseasoned legs
had yet to weave or waddle),
but now you can locomote
across our cedared deck
like a duck on rollers and honk
your horn like a gaffed goose
to clear the clutter, and in
your eyes is all the laughter
that fifteen months of loving
allows, and the grin you give me
is all pluck and unbeguiling
gumption.

Pop

The War and its faraway
horrors hollowed out
the fathers of my town, and the only
young men I noticed
had flat feet, a newly minted
limp or horn-rimmed
glasses an inch thick,
and so it was that our mothers
dumped us out-of-doors
with our breakfast still buoyant,
and we roamed the heathen streets
and combed the curbside
grasses for two-penny
empties and mimicked commandos
till the curfew quelled us,
and lucky was the lad with a
toy Tommy gun
going rat-a-tat-tat
and lolloping Jerries this way
and that, just like dad,
and casting about for mine,
I settled for calling my grandfather
"Pop."

Doing the Deed

After reading Cumming's
"Red rag pink flag"

At seventeen, I hadn't yet
done the deed or cadged
a girl to gift it, but I dreamt
of the day, this side
of Heaven, when love's cudgel,
with no regrets, would blood
some virgin's badge
and breed it.

Akin

Rondeau Park: July 1954

She was just an ordinary girl
we kibitzed with that summer
Saturday on Rondeau's tawny
sands, but the first one
of that silken ilk with an amorous
eye, and beamed at me
with uninhibited vim,
and when my tongue no longer
tripped on itself, I pitched
a bit of woo with words
I didn't know I knew,
and on the car-ride home,
we shared a rumble-seat,
a pair of rummaging lips
and the prim beginnings of some-
thing akin to lust.

Dubbed

I suppose that "Indian summer"
has been caught up in the woolly
web of the thought police,
as if there were something
seasonally illicit in the phrase,
reprising, as it does, the amber
autumnal afternoons
when Attawandaron combed
their dawn-washed woods
and clam-clattered beaches,
and let the last of the
summer light quicken the skin
and rub it roseate, and did not
care that colour-blind,
blue-eyed interlopers,
spotting their coppery hue,
dubbed them "Indians."

Dodgems

For Tim, at three

How many magic mornings
found us paired in your romper
room: you astride your plastic
tractor, playing dodgems
with me and whatever wall
was brave enough to bounce you
bug-eyed backwards,
and the "whee" you whooped was all
glee and grin, ringing
the rafters like Stompin' Tom
high on his booted flute,
and once again I thank
the good gods for their gift –
jolted ajar by joy
and the wonder of huggable love.

Forge

When I was almost two,
words still floated like flotsam
about the dizzied drum
in my ears, unattached to
anything that mattered, but when
they did so, their syllables sang
of infant selves and home,
and I gorged on the music of their meaning,
suspecting, even then,
that the limit of my lexicon would be
infinite, and any rhymes
to be forged in the fury of their flexing
would poem the world.

Munch

Once a week, my Gran
whips up a batch of peanut-
butter treats, and the word
on the street zooms beyond
our block and back, and kids
I know, and some I don't,
arrive on our pitched porch,
like bachelored bees on the honeyed
hive, or bibbed and dribbling
toddlers, fresh from the teat,
and as I sashay down
like a zoot-suited waiter
with an over-loaded tray
of just un-ovened cookies,
the air rings with a carnivore's
cry: "My dibs!" and when the
munching's done, not a crumb
survives – for man or God.

Gothic

In Leckie's barn, we feel
the hush of hay in manger
and mow, note the fluting
coo of pigeons somewhere
aloft and hear the breeze
of the milch-cows' breath
and the pleading bleat of a
newborn, on stilts in its stall,
and the resident owl, estranged
from light, rearranges
his scowl, and in the far
dark a bat unwraps,
and I think of cathedrals in their gothic
yaw and buttressed bellies,
and a place where prayers are soft
enough to be heard in Heaven.

Sufficient

February, 1961
for Anne in loving memory

When you answered *Yes*
to my romantic gambit,
I smiled so far inside
that my bones bounced, and you
said to calm my waters,
"I won't wear a diamond,"
and I knew even before
the nuptial niceties were done
that you'd be nobody's trophy
to be won or worshipped,
and I was happy just
to go ambling down the aisle
with you, certain that half-
a-loaf would more than suffice.

Eve's Dream

O the girls of the Point
seem to float from street
to street with long-limbed
vim and faery's feet,
their wimple-bibbed blouses
nippled by the wind, their tresses,
honey-blond or dappled
black, lay un-caressed
by a lover's touch or lust's
illicit bliss, and in
their blue-eyed gaze
lies Eve's dream of
Eden's green acre,
with a lurch in her loins
and an orchard of apples,
waiting to be plucked.

Close Shave

For Gary McCord

The butcher's brother, after a
Saturday booze-up in the *Balmoral,*
gathered all of his grievances
in one pot and looked about
for someone to beat besides
his wife, and there was Gary,
freckled and free and happily
hirsute, and before the lad
could say, "Don't, Dad!"
he was billiard-ball bald,
not a tuft left to flutter
or flaunt, but Gary had the
last un-embittered laugh:
he sashayed around town,
this way and that, without a hat.

Rites

Sarnia Collegiate: 1950-1951

We were thirty-three Grade
Niners, all male and posturing
testosterone, and at Assembly
we sat in the lofted loges
like a crouching cabal and sang
the nonsense ditty parlayed
on the screen, as if our lungs
wanted inside out, with the gusto
of a fractured fugue, and young
Gibson, the class cut-up,
would rise, at some self-
inflicted cue, and soliloquize
in song like a boogeying basso,
and for a while, singing along,
I could believe that loneliness
wasn't a character flaw
or that being bullied was not
a necessary rite of passage.

The Gift

For Anne in loving memory

The pelvic pouch was meant
to keep the foetus firmly
in, but doubled as a cradle
for my lust that softened it
into something akin to love,
and in the tender tangling
of our bodies and the enthused fusion
of our flesh was the world amazed
and we viewed it through the gift
of other's gaze.

Oldies A-Curling

For Bob Clark and Ken Cooper

The cry "Hurry hard!"
rattles the rink's rafters
like the ululation of a bit
Banshee, but there's little
hurry left in these geezers
or curl in their mottled locks
as they wobble-glide across
the allotted ice like inebriate
geese on an over-polished
pond – brooms a-thrashing
like teeth a-gnashing – as they try
to persuade a forty-pound
rock to behave and make
a shot for the skipper, and,
like elderly 'gamers' everywhere
dream, between a wince
and a wheeze, of days when the bat
shook hands with the ball
or granite with the pin, and they all
still had their hair.

Turf

Point Edward: July 1947

I remember well the Summer
morn when the sun shone
as if something mattered,
and my uncles – as bare-backed
as a pair of Roman palookas
fisting in the Forum, their bronzed
torsos weeping sweat –
carved lozenges of lawn
(as crisp as a jeweller's cut)
from Grandfather's sacred acre,
above the bobbing oblongs
of tile and all the way down
to the septic's scented receptacle,
buried beneath us like a
brigantine's bilge, and I wondered
how long before I grew
muscled enough to tussle
with turf, or disembody
sod, or question God's
allotments.

Aghast

Honeymoon Bay: July 1980

Beyond our mosquito-deeted
abode, the Bay is happily
lapping in the star-dotted
dark, and somewhere, afar,
a moon waits to be born
out of lunar light and cosmic
flotsam, and tucked in our love-
snug cocoon, we feel
the intragalactic grip
of the vast firmament above
that leaves us diminished/
ecstatic/aghast.

Nobody Home

With a nod to e.e.

Betty-and-Bill go hide-
and-seeking in the just-about
gloam, where the Bogeyman
breathes, and Wendy-and-Will
come tumbling after
with a flail of wayward pail,
and every boy-girl
who can dance its gender down
comes running aglow
to the whiff of whatever or the itch
of what-if, and somewhere afar
where tales are still told,
Rapunzel's bungee comes
undone for her lover's elastic
leap, and Cinderella
gets a slippered fit, and the fella,
and Hansel and Gretel settle
for gingerbread and a witch
in the oven, and Goldilocks
pots the porridge and sins
in triplicate, and the Billy-Goats
Gruff hoodwink a troll
in his toll-taking moat,
and the Pied Piper on his three-
hooved stance tootles
a child-beguiling air
and heads for Hamelin, and when
the "ollie-ollie-en-fray"
whistles far and wee,
Nobody's home.

Once-World

Unblessed by the bliss
or bother of a sister, I pictured
girls an alien species,
all frocks and fillies, tossed
locks and batted lashes,
with legs lithe enough
to be untroubled
by double-Dutch or "kneesies"
off-the-wall, and we were
justly gendered: marbles
for males and bounce-a-ball
a feminine fiefdom,
and our giddying games stayed
in their behooving grooves
till something shivered an id,
and boy-girls and their once-
world came wooing to grief.

Fandango

Point Edward: 1948
for Shirley McCord

Shirley does her fandango
on Grandfather's lawn,
her girl's body still
unbloomed, as lithe as a
willow bending in the breeze,
but in the hurly-burly
of her hips and the frantic prance
of her gams and the pelvic
pout of her lustrous lips
and the intimate glint her eyes
give out, something
of the woman's she's doomed
to be comes through –
a slow Venusian moon
igniting the sky.

Iridescence

Honeymoon Bay: July, 1980

That night, beside the breeze-
brushed Bay in the ghostly
gleam of a honeyed moon,
we lay like lovers, lost in the
hush of the other's awe,
too tender for touch
or the abrupt coupling of words,
happy to be here under
the aegis of the stars and the lapping
pentameter of wavelets on the
granite brim, letting
our bareboned loneliness
lapse, and our dreams irridesce.

Abelard to Heloise

O how we loved the roil
and writhe of our bodies' blundering
bliss – the holy grappling
of flesh to flesh, the slow
dozing aftermath, and the underwater
thunder that kept our rusted
lusts lithe, but now,
alas and apart, we must
memorialize our love in these
tender-petalled letters
that speak to the heart's ease
and keep our bliss epistolary,
until it climbs like roses
on a vestal vine, and soars.

A Bible Story

In a house where books were as rare
as pigeon's teeth, the only
stories I imbibed, beyond
those triplicate tales
of home-body bears,
impudent pigs and Billy-
goats tripping across
a bridge – the ones my grand-
father recited with nimble
mimicry and a bounce of the nearest
knee – were the lusty sagas
from *Stories of the Bible,* a lushly
coloured tome that was a gift
from my mother to keep me
literate and loving the Lord,
and I let them seethe like frenzied
bees and settle in the mind:
Adam and Eve, ungarnished
in the Garden; ageing Abe,
weighing the odds and God's
command; Joshua's trumpeting
harrumph that brought down
a town; Elijah, who took
the high road to Heaven
in fiery style; Lot's other,
who just had to have a last,
petrifying peek; Samson,
un-coifed and frazzled
in Gaza; Job, who could take
a punch and smile as if
a plague were persiflage;
David, who parlayed a pebble
and grounded a Goliath; Bathsheba,
prudently nuse, who took a king

to her blemished bed; Shadrack
and his best buds, fanning
the flames; Lazarus, who woke up
at home and wondered where he was;
Solomon, whose titillating hymn
to Hymen sang of the body
as as holy abode; and of course
there was Jesus, who stood
tall on Galilee just
because he could, and fed
the multitude with a lonesome
loaf and a fileted fish;
who died for the sins I had
yet to commit; and in
these sometimes tatter-
demalion tales, I found plots
enough (and the protagonists
peopling them) to paper
the world with my poems.

Abelard to Heloise

O how we loved the roil
and writhe of our bodies' blundering
bliss – the holy grappling
of flesh to flesh, the slow
dozing aftermath, and the underwater
thunder that kept our rusted
lusts lithe, but now,
alas and apart, we must
memorialize our love in these
tender-petalled letters
that speak to the heart's ease
and keep our bliss epistolary,
until it climbs like roses
on a vestal vine, and soars.

Laura

Chatham, Ontario: 1953

Laura Haggith, daughter
of my dad's best friend,
wore her jeans so tight
we could see, to our delight,
the crease in her crotch,
and her new-brandished breasts
slept erect beneath
a bevelled blouse, but I was
much taken with the smile
she tossed at me like a soft
summons or a laggard glance,
as if she had more than her body
to offer and would never be
just another notch
on anyone's amorous oar.

Diptych: Paradise

Eve's Bereavement

The fruit of that forbidden
tree must have tasted
juicy when Eve opted
for curiosity and the enthrall
of knowledge, and found herself
somewhere East of Eden,
prudely nude and fig-
leaved, surprised at God's
ferocity and the bite of her
bereavement.

Adam's Lapse

Adam was ever at ease
in Eden among the flowers
that bloomed till they didn't,
then bloomed again, pleased
to be his own God-
coddled companion, and when
his Lord ripped out a rib
and freed Eve, he felt
no ache in their nakedness
nor any inkling of id
at the sight of her perfect paps,
until that pondering consort
took a bite too far –

                    and he lapsed.

Lingo

In the Point we had our own
lingo, not quite the lexicon
of Shakespeare or Winnie,
but rather our way of naming
the world that grew us
and kept us ept: and so
the local drinking den
was always the Bal-morale
and Barr's Billiards just the
pool hall and the bulrushing
marsh was just our mosquito-
breeding swamp and the woodlot
where we walked our Sundays
along was First Bush
just because it was
and the indiscreetly-heaped
garbage pits were just
Dunham's dump and the plinthed
Cenotaph was just the monument
on which kids gambolled when school
was not and the Blue Water
cantilevered beauty was just
the bridge and the Saharan sweep
of Canatara where silicone
tingled our toes was just
the beach and its Park just
a place for picnics among
the hundred-year oaks
and the City Golf Club
that sprawled obscenely green
across our borders was just
the lawn for doctors walking
their Wednesdays – and these
homely monikers and heartfelt
appellations were bestowed
with friendly affection and the
ballast of belonging.

Banana Split / Two Bits

Around the corner from the *Park*
where six-gun Saturdays
featured Hopalong or Johnny
Mack in sagebrush sagas
full of manufactured
fury and improbable posses,
lay the *Dairy Bar,*
where for a nickel or its nudge
we could sip on a malted shake
till the straws exhausted,
while watching, with eminent envy,
the soda-pop jockey
concocting banana-splits
with three oozing scoops
of vanilla and a thin drizzle
of chocolate, topped with a
sneeze of peanuts and matching
maraschinos – and I wondered
aloud how long it might be
before I found a quarter,
pulsing in my pocket, or felt
my candied appetite budge.

Buttered Bread

Point Edward: 1948

Butch and I, tucked
in the back room of his father's
shop, "licking" ration-
stamps (brown for meat,
mauve for butter, grey
for tea, et cetera) and pasting them
prettily upon government-
numbered sheets ("Going
straight to Parliament Hill,"
we're told) until our thumbs
numb, our single Sunday
Pepsi sipped til' the bottom
dropped, its twin straws
exhausted, and looking again
at the mauve kind, I wonder
aloud what in the world
Mister King would do with all
that butter, and echoing his dad's
delivery, Butch replies
with evident pride, "He butters
his bread on both sides."

Enough

For Tom in loving memory

My grief has broken out again
like a burst boil, its pain
like a bud too blooded
to bloom, and I know
we all love at our peril
and loss is the price we pay
for bidding our soul be severed
and bound to another's, for daring
the gods at their own ado,
but still, we relish the roil
of such intimate collisions,
such transfusions of touch,
and so it is, I stoke
the coals of what remains
of the love we shared, that soared
sunward, above the buffering
stars – and that is enough.

Taking No Chances

Point Edward: 1947

When the Reverend Bell's manse
blew up, as if some
artful arsonist, with a grievance
against God, had planted
a bomb in the kitchen and hung
around to watch the cutlery
fly, the good parson,
whose misanthropic match
had set the tinder alight,
(surprised to be still alive),
teetered a while on his meta-
tarsals, and offered his thanks
to the Lord in flawless Latin
and, taking no chances,
repeated them in hackneyed
vernacular.

Sailing with the Wind

For Bruce Ashdown in loving memory

You always sailed with the wind –
at the punters' wicket or on
the seventh sea, a blustering
breeze ever bellying
your jib, the tiller, a wizard's
wand in your fist: you rode
the incoming, ravenous rollers
like a bos'un's mate on skis
or a bibbed babe, skittering
on skates, and hydroplaned
your ark upon the beckoning
beach like a dove-guided
Noah, juddering the sands
of Ararat, your skipper's grin
as wide as Ahab's, withering
a whale.

Parables of Snow

Ever since I first
perused Ned Pratt's
"Sea Gulls," I've wanted
to pen a poem entitled
"Parables of Snow," for which
I hoped to cull suitable
similes from my treasury of tropes,
but the Muse refused to go
along, and sent me instead
in search of some ground
more arable.

Tinge

For Jim French

You wrote your own auto-
biography by living your life
out loud and leaving nothing
in the silence behind un-
forgotten, and the words you wrought
of your sojourn abroad in the seething
Tanzanian heat or those
cozy hours of home
and filial affection (too soon
abrupted) or your love-fraught
high-schooling days
tell the story of a man
and pedagogue with poetry
in his soul (and a penchant for the ponies),
with something ever at ease
inside, thinned with a tinge
of the rowdy.

Alvin

Chatham, Ontario: July 1953
For Alvin Gehl in loving memory

You weren't exactly Huck
Finn, but the gimcrack raft
you cobbled out of withered wood
and wobbly logs, had pluck
enough to keep you afloat,
and skeptics all, we watched you
poling your jerry-rigged
craft primly along the
mud-freckled Thames
with a grin on your face that said,
"Look, Ma! Here I am
and I can't even swim."

George

For George Martell in loving memory

You doffed your academic
robes and prowled the picket
lines, braving the wince
of Winter or the heave of Summer's
heat, for you believed
in the lofty principles you preached,
becoming the voice of inner-
city kids, too often
mute, and pinched by poverty
and malign neglect, or made
the object of every do-
gooding gambit on the block,
and you were ever careless
of scoffers or the knowing wink,
bearing the burden of a famous
father and a warmth that wept
when a poem punctured or a painting
purred, and O how I miss
the long-range, soul-
probing conversations
we shared for more than a decade,
like a pair of Aristotelian
lingo-phobes.

Helter-Skelter

When summer storms rolled in
unthrottled from the throat
of our Great Lake, we dashed
outdoors, bathing-suited
and bare of foot, squelching
the saturate grass, paying
no heed to the rain's rage
or the wind's welter, for we
were young and far too
immortal to be bothered
or have our helter-skelter
ways succumbed.

Moon-Mad

Point Edward: 1947

Mara's lamp, the only
light along Monck,
drew us to its amber ambience
like moths to something molten
or bats to a beam, and beyond it
lay the star-harbouring
dark, where the Bogeyman breathed
agley, and undeterred, we went
hide-and-go-seeking and home-
free into its furred fathoms,
and let our moon-mad
bodies be.

Hockey Heroes

Charlie Levin, Bill
Mara and my father made up
the 'Kid Line' who parlayed
their rink-wizardry into a
kind of fame that brought
the locals frantic to their feet
and put the giddy in the gals'
gams, but barely old enough
to vote or imbibe, and chuffed
by cheers and tears, they went
willingly off to the wars
and worse, and when they came
back home, battle-bruised,
Levin and Mara took
a year and drank their demons
to death, and my Dad waited
forty-some years to do
the same: Hockey Heroes
all, whom fame couldn't save,
un-applauded in their graves.:

My Boy

For Tom in loving memory

Two years since you've been gone,
and the wound still weeps,
and when you left us, you took
some part of the world's
joy with you, and what little
remained for me tasted
too much of loss and bitter
might-have-beens to hoist
the heart above the ballast
of its beating, but even so,
the blood will seek some solace
in the flurry of its flowing
and our bones bend on the iron
lust of love, and it's enough,
surely, to rejoice in these
simple truths, and say
your name aloud: my boy,
my beautiful, blue-eyed
Tom.

Aplomb

I devoured *Tom Sawyer*
before the Christmas tree
gave up, stirred
by a story of boyhood bravado
and Polly-antic antics,
then hurried on to *Huck Finn*
with its jaundiced jaunt down the
Mississip on a gimcrack
raft with saucer-eyed
Jim abaft, and I prayed
that any Territory found
be rippled free of bigots
and Bible-thumping drummers –
and I didn't know which
I liked better: Huck's pluck
or Tom's aplomb.

Halo

For Anne in loving memory

Four years have passed
since last I wisped a wayward
curl from your brow or lingered
long upon your lips
or hugged you snug in my bravo-
embrace, .and there was always
something holy in your soul,
un-martyred and merciful,
that left me aglow – with a
halo round my heart.

Below the Bridge

Point Edward: 1948

Down below the Bridge
in the bog, where bullfrogs
in the croaking throe of their throats
are making a rueful music
and bulrushes are brushed hirsute
by the breeze, and water-lilies
un-wizen in the sun and marsh
marigolds glow golden
and a bobolink sings, like a
minstrel on his lute, the syllables
of his name in rippling triplicate –
Butch and I pass merely
by without a nod or a wink
to the gods who dreamed this peaceable
place and let it be,
intent as we are in thrashing
the grasses agog in hopes
of startling a harmless garter
and watching it twitch away
like Lucifer exiting Eden,
and something in the soul
of this setting redeems
our casual passing and wakens us
to the ripe ritual of the day.

Purr

When Adam knew their nakedness
and felt the first lurch
of his loins at Eve's teasing
demur, he purloined a lotus
leaf to brighten her brow,
and spoke not a word as he honeyed
a vowel and stroked her posey
till she purred.

Stories

For my mother in loving memory

There were no books
in Grandfather's abode,
upstairs or down, but during
the War, when nights were long
in the curtained dark, my mother,
alone with two toddlers
and her thoughts, perused her way
through a shelf-and-a-half
of bloated tomes from our little
library (tucked above
the jail) before the nine
o'clock curfew shuttered
the town, and I watched her reading
from my invalid's bed, her lips
moving to the fictive rhythms
on the page, and I wondered, even then,
if the stories she inhaled
might heal the lesions of her loneliness.

Stuffed

For my father in loving memory

My Dad, among his divers
talents, took up
taxidermy, learning
from a book, page by patient
page, how to parse arsenic
and supple a killed creature's
inside skin, and bring
its body abrupt to life
with all of its animal stance
intact – except for Fox's
caustic stare, combing
his element, or Coon's two-
mooned midnight glancing,
or Gray-Wolf's toxic gawk,
but try as I might, I could see
nothing in the glass-eyed
gazes that came my way,
or in my father's resurrecting
bent, but something gutted
and stuffed.

A Deviant Day

Point Edward: 1947

I well remember the June
afternoon when the sky
above the rim of our Lake
became clotted with cloud,
cumulo-nimbal blooms
whose bloated bellies presaged
something more menacing
than rain, and when the air
cooled around us like a gelid
jacket, it was blurred with flurries
that glistened the grass, and some-
where, the Earth's certainties
shook — and I found that deviant
day as odd as a boneless
body or a crooked nook
or an un-Apostled God.

Boreal

On his first day in Paradise,
before the advent of Eve,
Adam had time to apprise
the greenery and wonder which god
could have wrought it so,
but all that changed when Eve
arrived, estranged from her borrowed
body and bored with things
arboreal, fraternized with the
Fruit Forbidden, grew
naughtily nude and dabbled
in a bit of obscene-ery.

Venusian

Point Edward: 1948
for Shirley McCord

Shirley does her fan dance
on Grandfather's lawn,
her girl's body still
unbloomed, as lithe as a
willow bending in the breeze,
but in the hurly-burly
of her hips and the frantic prance
of her gams and the pelvic
pout of her lustrous lips
and the intimate glint her eyes
give out, something
of the woman she's doomed
to be comes through —
a slow Venusian moon
igniting the sky.

Gambler

It may have been Bonnie
who suggested Strip Poker
that day, but I was an instant
gunslinging gambler,
and five hands on,
Bonnie was down to her last
decent dud, and when I
turned up a pair of deuces,
she smiled with shy surmise,
and let her pink pantaloons
slink, ooze and puddle
on her toes, and I was too
befuddled at the sight of her budding
rose, winking my way,
to cash in my chips.

Welter

During the War (I knew
only from the absence of the father
I was said to have somewhere
in the alien air beyond
my loving and lofting over
Labrador), I watched
my grandfather in tunic blue
and brass put his young
cadets through their paces
in the high school gym,
and never once did he glance up
at me and my adoring eyes,
and I wondered whether, in that
inner ear which never
leaves us, he could still hear
the hum of bombs, flung
in random rage above
the killing fields of the Somme,
and prayed those lads
would find some other way
to test their mettle or justify
their being than in the fratricidal
welter of war.

Don Gutteridge was born in Sarnia and raised in the nearby village of Point Edward. He taught High School English for seven years, later becoming a Professor in the Faculty of Education at Western University, where he is now Professor Emeritus. He is the author of more than seventy books: poetry, fiction and scholarly works in pedagogical theory and practice. He has published twenty-two novels, including the twelve-volume Marc Edwards mystery series, and forty-nine books of poetry, one of which, Coppermine, was short-listed for the 1973 Governor-General's Award. In 1970 he won the UWO President's Medal for the best periodical poem of that year, "Death at Quebec." Don lives in London, Ontario.

Email: gutteridgedonald@gmail.com.